Aural Time!

Practice Tests for the New Revised ABRSM Syllabus and Other Exams

Grade 6

DAVID TURNBULL

CONTENTS

Published by
Bosworth & Co. Limited
14-15 Berners Street,
London W1T 3LJ, UK.

Exclusive Distributors:
Music Sales Limited
Distribution Centre, Newmarket Road,
Bury St Edmunds, Suffolk IP33 3YB, UK.
Music Sales Pty Limited
20 Resolution Drive, Caringbah,
NSW 2229, Australia.

This book © Copyright 2010 Bosworth.
International Copyright Secured.

Printed in the EU.

Unauthorised reproduction of any part of this
publication by any means including photocopying is an
infringement of copyright.

BOSWORTH
part of The Music Sales Group

INTRODUCTION

Having had the privilege of working with the late David Turnbull on a number of his projects, including the original publication of some of the *Aural Time!* volumes, it is a great pleasure to contribute to this new edition of his work, which takes account of various mainly small revisions to the aural tests of the Associated Board of the Royal Schools of Music examinations, effective from January 2011 onwards.

At Grade 6 the following changes have been made, all of which are reflected in this book:

- In Tests A and B, excerpts are now restricted to key signatures of no more than three sharps or flats, and the part to be sung by candidates is now limited to a range of an octave.

- In Test C, candidates are no longer required to identify the key as major or minor – they only have to identify the cadence at the end of the passage as perfect or imperfect.

- In Test D (i), questions will be limited to two features of the music, the first on texture or phrase structure, and the second on another element (excluding rhythm, although candidates will still have to clap a rhythm from the piece in part (ii) of the test). In questions on the character of the music, candidates will be expected to identify specific musical features of the piece to support their views.

As teachers, many of us have pupils who love performing but who are daunted by aural tests, and who sadly see otherwise excellent examination marks reduced by weakness in this area. The reason is often because aural skills are left until the final lessons before an exam. It is essential not to see aural perception as a 'bolt-on' extra but as fundamental to good music making. For example, Test C in Grade 6 could be related to the music that pupils enjoy – can they hear how an imperfect cadence signals to the listener that there is more to come, while a perfect cadence creates a feeling that a musical statement has run its course? Similarly, questions on style and character in Test D can often be related to the set pieces the pupil is learning.

At Grade 6, the first two tests require a sung response (although it is well worth remembering that candidates can opt to play instead of sing in Test A). Those who worry about singing should be reassured that tone doesn't matter – they can hum or whistle if they prefer – it is only pitch and rhythm that are assessed. The part to be sung will lie within a range of an octave and candidates may tell the examiner the range within which they prefer to sing if they wish. Pupils may find another book in the *Aural Time!* series useful in preparation for Test B. *Easy Sight Singing & Voice Pitching Practice*, (Bosworth Edition 4801), contains 70 short examples of accompanied sight-singing suitable for a beginner, in a variety of major and minor keys.

Pupils need to be secure in the technical vocabulary likely to be encountered in Test D. In particular, they should understand that 'tonality' refers to the use of keys in the piece (major, minor, modulations from one key to another, and so on) – it is nothing to do with the tone colour of the music. Equally, 'texture' relates to the ways in which simultaneous layers of a passage of music relate to each other – the term is not a synonym for dynamics or articulation. Pupils also need to be clear on how they should justify their views on the character (and, if required, the style and period) of the music played in Test D by referring to specific musical features of the piece. Study of the commentaries at the end of this book will show the type of responses that could be made to Test D questions although these are not, of course, the only possible answers.

Paul Terry,
London 2010

Uniform with this volume: *Aural Time!* Grades 1–5 and 7–8.

Also by David Turnbull: *Theory Time!* Step-by-step instruction in musical theory and rudiments. Grades 1–5.

All published by Bosworth & Co.

1   Test A. Singing or Playing from Memory

Pupils must sing or play from memory the upper part of a two-part phrase. The key-chord and the starting note will be played and named, and two bars of the pulse will be tapped.

In an examination, the example will be played twice. When giving practice, however, teachers should not hesitate to play the test more frequently, and if necessary be prepared to divide the test into sections. Tests should be played at the keyboard using both hands, so that the separate lines are as clearly defined as possible. *If the example starts with a single part or a unison, the pupil must be warned.*

3

4

2 Test B. Sight-Singing

Pupils must sing a short melody from score, with an accompaniment being played for them. The key-chord and starting note will be sounded, and the pulse indicated. Grade 6 sight-singing can be in any major or minor key up to three sharps or three flats. In an examination, pupils may choose to sing either in the treble or the bass clef. When practising, however, pupils are advised to familiarise themselves with both clefs, singing the examples up or down an octave as necessary.

10

Ford: *Since first I saw your face*

5   **Andante**

Torelli: *Tu lo sai*

6   **Andante**

Byrd: *My Little Sweet Darling*

7   **Lento**

Trad: *Blow the wind southerly*

8   **Lento**

12

13

Slow

Purcell: *Dido and Aeneas*

21

Andante

Cavalli: *Dolce amor bendato Dio*

22

Tempo moderato

Bach: *Christmas Oratorio*

23

Larghetto ma non troppo

Gounod: *O Salutaris*

24

Moderato

Handel: *See the Conquering Hero Comes*

Allegretto

Lotti: *Par dicesti*

Moderato

Fauré: *Requiem*

Allegro

Purcell: *Man is for the Woman made*

Purcell: *Aeolus' Song*

Handel: *Messiah*

Weber: *Der kleine Fritz an seine jungen Freunde*

Schubert: *Der König in Thule*

Allegro

Schubert: *Who is Sylvia?*

53

Largo ma non troppo

Handel: *Messiah*

54

Monteverdi: *Lasciatemi morire*

55

Fauré: *Requiem*

56

3 Test C. Perfect and Imperfect Cadences.

(Pupils are advised to read over pages 20 – 21 of Theory Time! *Grade 5)*

In Grade 6 aural tests, pupils need only to be able to recognise **perfect and imperfect cadences**. A **perfect cadence** ends with the tonic chord, preceded by the dominant (or the dominant seventh) chord. An **imperfect cadence** ends with the dominant chord, preceded by any other chord. To be successful in Grade 6 cadence tests, pupils must be able to decide quickly if a phrase ends on the tonic chord (in which case the cadence is perfect), or on the dominant chord (in which case the cadence is imperfect).

In **major** keys, the tonic and dominant chords are both major chords. In **minor** keys, the tonic chord is minor, but the dominant chord is *major*. In Grade 6 tests, therefore, if a passage in a minor key ends with a major chord *the cadence must be imperfect.*

The key chord will always be sounded before a phrase is played over, so the pupil will know if the key of the phrase is major or minor. Teachers should ensure that the keychord is recognised correctly before continuing with the test.

A number of examples contain two cadences for identification. In some of these cases, the final chord of the first cadence is marked with a pause sign (fermata).

26

4   Test D. Questions about Pieces

In Test D of ABRSM examinations the questions on pieces are in two parts.

D (i)   Pupils should be able to answer two questions about the **musical features** of a piece. The first will be on texture or structure, the second will be on one of the following: dynamics, articulation, tempo, tonality, character, style and period, texture/structure.

Before playing the music, tell the pupil which two features the questions will be about (e.g. 'Listen to this short piece, then I'll ask you about texture [or structure] and [name the second feature you have chosen]'). For practice purposes, a selection of questions is provided for each of the examples that follow.

Comments on the questions about pieces in this section are printed on Page 38.

D (ii)   Pupils should be able to clap the rhythm of a short extract from the same piece, and describe it as being in two, three, or four time (they are not required to state the time signature). In examinations, candidates will only be asked to clap one example, but to provide more practice two examples for clapping are given for each of the pieces below.

The questions in this section are useful preparation for many other types of music examination, such as GCSE and A-level. Pupils for other examinations can practise writing down answers instead of giving them verbally.

D (i)   *Questions*

(a)   **Texture**: Is the texture of this piece homophonic (block chords), or contrapuntal?
(b)   **Texture**: Comment on the relationship between the melody and bass at the start of the music.
(c)   **Tonality**: What can you say about the tonality of this music?
(d)   **Tempo**: Does the tempo alter, or stay the same throughout?
(e)   **Dynamics**: Briefly describe the use of dynamics in this piece.
(f)   **Articulation**: What musical term describes the way the notes are articulated in this music?

D (ii)   Clap one of the following extracts, and say if it is in two, three or four time.

Tempo di Menuetto

William Shield

D (i) *Questions*

(a) **Structure**: Describe the phrase structure of this piece.
(b) **Texture**: Is the texture of the music contrapuntal or homophonic?
(c) **Tempo**: Does the speed of the music alter, or stay the same?
(d) **Tonality**: Briefly describe the tonality of this piece.
(e) **Style and period**: In which historical period might this piece have been written?

D (ii) Clap one of the following extracts, and say if it is in two, three or four time.

Andante   Bach

D (i) *Questions*

(a) **Structure**: Comment on the structure of the melody in the first half of this piece.
(b) **Structure**: How long are most of the phrase lengths in this piece?
(c) **Texture**: What musical term best describes the texture of this music?
(d) **Tempo**: Does the tempo vary during the piece, or does it stay the same?
(e) **Tonality**: Is the tonality mostly major, or mostly minor? Does it change?
(f) **Articulation**: How are the notes articulated in this piece?

D (ii) Clap one of the following extracts, and say if it is in two, three or four time.

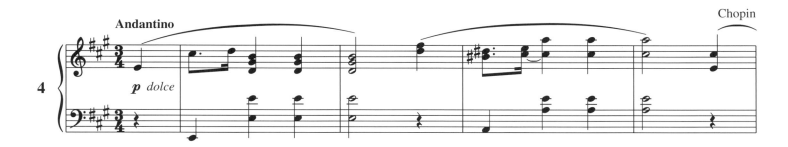

D (i) *Questions*

(a) **Structure**: What do you notice about the phrase structure of this piece?

(b) **Texture**: Is the texture of this piece homophonic (block chords), or polyphonic (contrapuntal)?

(c) **Tempo**: Does the tempo alter during the piece? If so, how?

(d) **Dynamics**: Describe the **dynamics** of the piece.

(e) **Character**: What in the music gives this piece its character?

(f) **Style and period**: In what period might this piece have been written? What in the music suggests that period?

D (ii) Clap one of the following extracts, and say if it is in two, three or four time.

D (i) *Questions*

(a)   **Texture**: What can you say about the texture of this music?
(b)   **Structure**: This piece has three main phrases. How are they similar?
(c)   **Tonality**: Briefly describe the tonality of the music.
(d)   **Tempo**: What Italian term could be used to describe the tempo of this music?
(e)   **Articulation**: Explain how the articulation briefly changes shortly before the final cadence.
(f)   **Character**: What do you feel is the character of this piece?
(g)   **Style and period**: In what period might this music have been written?
      Which features in the music suggest that period?

D (ii)   Clap one of the following extracts, and say if it is in two, three or four time.

D (i) *Questions*

(a) **Texture**: Is this music mostly contrapuntal, or mostly homophonic?

(b) **Texture**: Comment on how the texture builds to a total of four parts in the first half of the piece.

(c) **Tempo**: Does the speed change at any point? If so, where?

(d) **Style and period**: This music was written in the baroque period. What in the music tells you that?

D (ii) Clap one of the following extracts, and say if it is in two, three or four time.

Avec une élégance grave et lent

Debussy

D (i) *Questions*

(a)   **Structure**: Is the opening phrase repeated exactly or can you identify any changes?

(b)   **Texture**: The opening is chordal. How does the texture change after the first two phrases?

(c)   **Tempo**: Does the tempo alter? If so, how?

(d)   **Character**: What in the music gives this piece its character?

(e)   **Dynamics**: What happens to the dynamics at the end?

(f)   **Style and period**: In what period might this have been written?

D (ii) Clap one of the following extracts, and say if it is in two, three or four time.

Tarrega

D (i)   *Questions*

(a)   **Texture**: Briefly comment on the texture of this piece.
(b)   **Structure**: How does the phrase structure suggest that this piece is a dance?
(c)   **Tonality**: Explain as precisely as you can how the tonality changes in the second half of the piece.
(d)   **Tempo**: Describe any variations that occur in the pulse of the music.
(e)   **Dynamics**: Where precisely is the loudest part of this piece?
(f)   **Style and period**: In what period might this music have been written?

D (ii) Clap one of the following extracts, and say if it is in two, three or four time.

D (i) *Questions*

(a) **Texture**: Describe the texture used throughout most of this piece.
(b) **Articulation**: Is the articulation of the notes legato, staccato, or a mixture of both?
(c) **Tempo**: Does the speed vary? If so, where?
(d) **Tonality**: Describe the tonality of this piece.
(e) **Style and period**: In what musical period do you think this music was written?

D (ii) Clap one of the following extracts, and say if it is in two, three or four time.

Andante teneramente

Brahms

D (i) *Questions*

(a) **Texture**: Comment on the difference in texture between the two halves of the piece.
(b) **Tonality**: How does the key in the second half of the piece relate to the key in the first half?
(c) **Tempo**: Describe any variations in speed during the piece.
(d) **Dynamics**: Briefly describe the dynamics in the piece.
(e) **Style and period**: What in the music indicates that this piece was written in the romantic period?

D (ii) Clap one of the following extracts, and say if it is in two, three or four time.

5 Appendix. Comments on the questions on music in Test D.

The answers below are not the only possible ones.

No. 1 (a) Contrapuntal; (b) the bass imitates the melody (an octave lower); (c) it is in a minor key throughout; (d) the tempo slows at the close of the second phrase and again at the end; (e) there are gradual changes in dynamics but none of the piece is very loud; (f) legato.

No. 2 (a) There are four main phrases, the third of which differs from the other three (AABA); (b) homophonic; (c) as score; (d) it is in a major key, with a modulation (to the dominant) in the second half; (e) straightforward harmony, homophonic texture, lack of dissonance and balance of phrases all suggest the classical period.

No. 3 (a) The four phrases are very similar apart from their endings (A, A^1, A, A^1); (b) 3 bars; (c) homophonic (melody and accompaniment); (d) it stays the same; (e) mostly major but with modulations (to the relative minor and to the dominant); (f) they are played legato.

No. 4 (a) All phrases are the same length/have the same rhythm/begin with an anacrusis; (b) homophonic; (c) as score; (d) as in score; (e) song-like melody, fairly slow tempo, dotted rhythm near the start of every phrase, waltz-like accompaniment patterns; (f) frequent use of 7th chords, gradations in dynamics, song-like melodic line, waltz-style accompaniment, and rallentando with pause at the climax all suggest the romantic period.

No. 5 (a) It consists of a melody accompanied by (mainly two-part) chords; (b) they each begin with the same dotted rhythm and they are all the same length; (c) minor key (with some chromatic writing in the middle section); (d) andante; (e) an ascending broken chord is played staccato; (f) quiet and a little melancholy, fairly slow but with a gently lilting rhythm; (g) classical period, suggested by periodic phrasing, melody-dominated texture (with appoggiaturas and other decoration of the melody), functional harmony with occasional chromatic writing, and use of the cadential second inversion.

No. 6 (a) Contrapuntal (four-part counterpoint); (b) each part enters in turn, from high to low, in imitation of the opening melody; (c) no; (d) the consistently contrapuntal (polyphonic) texture, crisp articulation, use of imitation, limited dynamic variety and straightforward harmony.

No. 7 (a) there is a small change at the start of the repeat and the dynamic level increases in mid-phrase, but otherwise it is the same; (b) it changes to bare octaves (a monophonic texture); (c) there is just a slight slowing down at the end; (d) thick, rich chords (particularly parallel 7ths), modal harmonies, restrained dynamics, a slow triple metre, often with a stress on the second beat of the bar (sarabande rhythm); (e) the dynamics fade to an almost imperceptible level; (f) all the foregoing features suggest late 19th/early 20th century.

No. 8 (a) A melody with chordal accompaniment, the texture becomes a little thicker in the second half; (b) the phrases are all of equal length (four bars) – as in most dance music, regular phrase lengths help dancers fit their steps to the music; (c) it changes to the tonic major; (d) the music slows down at the end of the first half and again in the middle of the second half, there is also a pause shortly before the final cadence; (e) just before the final cadence (at the pause); (f) all the foregoing answers, along with features such as the dominant 13th and augmented 6th chords, suggest the romantic period.

No. 9 (a) Melody with a broken chord (Alberti-bass) accompaniment; (b) a mixture of *legato* and *staccato*; (c) once, before the first very high quick notes; (d) major key, with brief modulations to related keys (dominant and subdominant); (e) functional harmony, lack of counterpoint, balanced phrases and the Alberti-style accompaniment all suggest the classical period.

No. 10 (a) In the first half, the melody is supported by arpeggios, while in the second half it is harmonised with dense block chords; (b) it is in the tonic (or parallel) major key; (c) as in score; (d) as in score; (e) flowing melodic line, rich harmonies, cross rhythms (the duplets against triplets in the first half), tempo fluctuations, use of both pedals on the piano.

Music engraving and typesetting by Musonix